MAPS & MAPMAKERS

MAPS & MAPMAKERS

How Maps Are Made

Martyn Bramwell

Illustrated by George Fryer

Lerner Publications Company • Minneapolis

This edition published in 1998

Lerner Publications Company
241 First Avenue North
Minneapolis MN 55401

Printed in Italy by Vallardi Industrie Grafich s.p.a.
Bound in the United States of America

Library of Congress Cataloging-in-Publication Data

Bramwell, Martyn.
     How maps are made / by Martyn Bramwell.
        p.   cm. – (Maps & mapmakers)
     Includes index.
     Summary: Describes the history of mapmaking and provides
instructions for making maps.
     ISBN 0-8225-2920-3 (lib. bdg.)
     1. Cartography–Juvenile literature. [1. Cartography. 2. Maps.]
I. Title. II. Series: Bramwell, Martyn. Maps & mapmakers.
GA105.6.B73   1998
526–dc21   97-10366

Acknowledgments

Thanks to The British Museum for the use of the picture bottom left on page 10;
Sokkia Ltd, Crewe, U.K. for use of the photograph used on page 35; Harper-
Collins Publishers Ltd, Glasgow, UK, for providing the photographs used on
pages 36-39; Aerofilms for supplying the photographs on pages 40-41; Scan-Globe
AS, Havdrup, Denmark, for the photographs on page 45; and Replogle Globes
Inc., Broadview, Ill., and Hubbard Scientific, Chippewa Falls, Wisconsin, for
additional advice.

Contents

Introduction

Just about anywhere we go, there are maps, or pictures, to help us find our way. Maps provide us with pictures of the earth's surface and the things on it, such as cities, roads, rivers, and mountains. By looking at a map, we can find out exactly where we are and how far it is from one place to another. On some maps we can see the shapes of the continents and oceans–shapes only an astronaut can look at in real life.

Some maps give us a picture of just a small part of the earth's surface, such as the town or village we live in. Others show bigger areas, such as a state or a country or even the whole world. It all depends on the **scale** of the map–the number of miles on the earth's surface that are represented by each inch on the map.

A single map can never show everything, so we use different maps for different purposes. Some give us a picture of the landscape–its hills and valleys, rivers and forests. Others indicate roads and railroad lines, important buildings, and interesting places to visit. Some show the kind of crops that are grown in a country or the number of people that live in an area. Each kind of map uses its own **key**–a set of colors and symbols that present information.

The first maps were simple drawings of coastlines and the position of important cities sketched by travelers and explorers. But as time went on, people learned how to draw much more accurate maps. Once they learned that the earth was round, they invented **map projections**, which enabled mapmakers to draw the earth's curved surface on flat sheets of paper. Later still, people invented special scientific instruments to measure distances, heights, and directions. Modern **cartographers**, or mapmakers, use radar, laser beams, aerial photographs, and satellites to measure features on the earth's surface and computers to help draw the maps.

The World as a Globe

For a long time, people thought the earth was flat. Around 250 B.C., the ancient Greeks realized our planet must be round. They studied the way the planets and stars traveled across the night sky. These heavenly bodies would disappear over the horizon and then reappear the next evening. That can only happen if you are watching them from the surface of a sphere that is spinning around and around. Another clue was the way ships would vanish over the horizon as they sailed away.

The best way to draw a picture of a round earth is to use another round object called a globe. But first we need some way of saying exactly where we are on the globe.

Positions on a globe are described using **latitude** and **longitude** lines. Lines of latitude, also called parallels, go around the earth, parallel to the equator. The equator lies at 0° latitude. Longitude lines, also called meridians, stretch north to south, from pole to pole, and look like the segments of an orange. The main reference line, at 0° longitude, is the Greenwich meridian, which runs through a suburb of London, England. The two sets of lines cross one another and form a kind of net, called a **grid**, that covers the entire globe. Using these numbered lines, we can describe exactly where a place is on the globe.

Axis
The imaginary line the earth spins around is called the axis. It is tilted, so globes are mounted at the same angle.

The Real Thing

Space research programs have provided some of the most beautiful photographs ever seen of the earth. With the sun's light reflecting off the clouds and the atmosphere, the planet shines brightly. Weather systems swirl across the surface, and parts of the continents and oceans can be seen through gaps in the clouds.

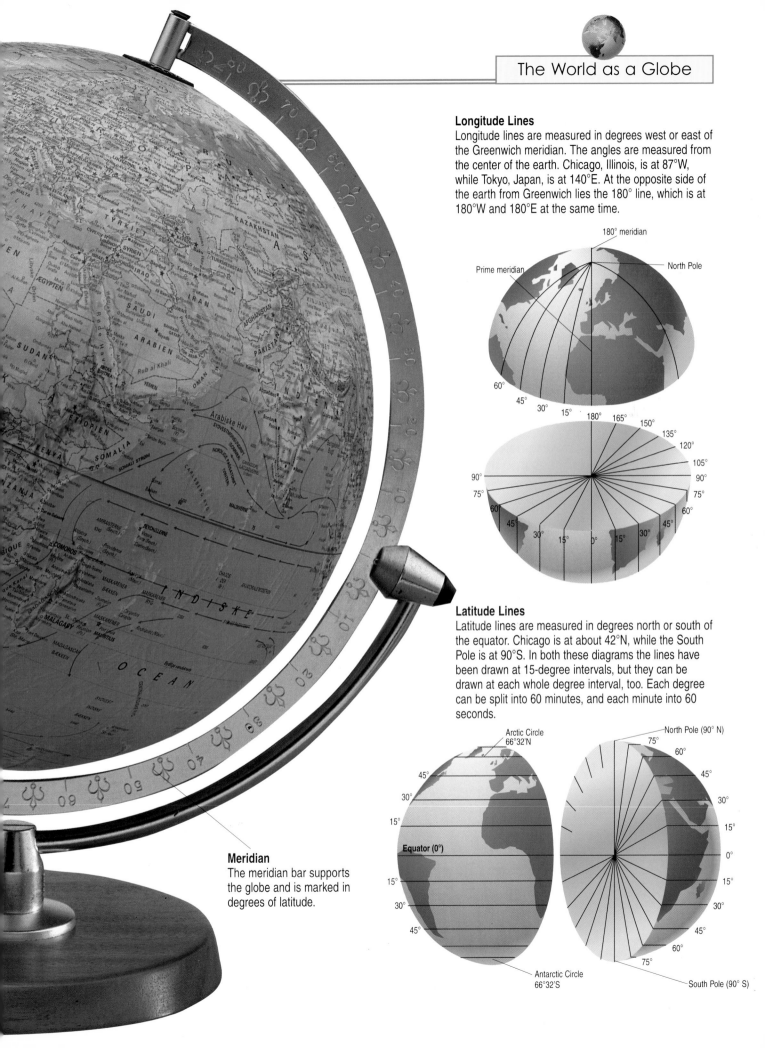

Longitude Lines

Longitude lines are measured in degrees west or east of the Greenwich meridian. The angles are measured from the center of the earth. Chicago, Illinois, is at 87°W, while Tokyo, Japan, is at 140°E. At the opposite side of the earth from Greenwich lies the 180° line, which is at 180°W and 180°E at the same time.

180° meridian

Prime meridian

North Pole

60°
45° 30° 15° 180° 165° 150°
135°
120°
105°
90° 90°
75° 75°
60° 60°
45° 45°
30° 15° 0° 15° 30°

Latitude Lines

Latitude lines are measured in degrees north or south of the equator. Chicago is at about 42°N, while the South Pole is at 90°S. In both these diagrams the lines have been drawn at 15-degree intervals, but they can be drawn at each whole degree interval, too. Each degree can be split into 60 minutes, and each minute into 60 seconds.

Arctic Circle
66°32'N

North Pole (90° N)

75°
60°
45° 45°
30° 30°
15° 15°
Equator (0°) 0°
15° 15°
30° 30°
45° 45°
60°
75°

Antarctic Circle
66°32'S

South Pole (90° S)

Meridian

The meridian bar supports the globe and is marked in degrees of latitude.

The First Maps

The oldest maps found so far date back to around 2500 B.C. They were made in Babylonia, which is now part of Iraq. Engraved on sturdy clay, these maps have survived for 4,500 years. Most are simple, sketched maps showing fields and villages, sometimes with rivers and hills nearby.

The First Great Mapmakers

The ancient Greeks were skilled mapmakers. By the fifth and sixth centuries B.C., they were mapping the Mediterranean Sea, Europe, and large parts of Asia and Africa–the whole world as they knew it. Ancient Greek maps are remarkably accurate considering that in those days people traveled on foot or by horse, camel, or boat and had no scientific instruments for measuring distances.

The most famous Greek mapmaker was Ptolemy, a brilliant astronomer and geographer who lived in the second century A.D. Ptolemy understood that the earth was round and wrote books about the theory of map projections. His map of the world, complete with lines of latitude and longitude, was so good that it was copied over and over again in the following centuries. Luckily for us, this famous map was finally published in a series of German atlases, more than 1,300 years after it had been drawn.

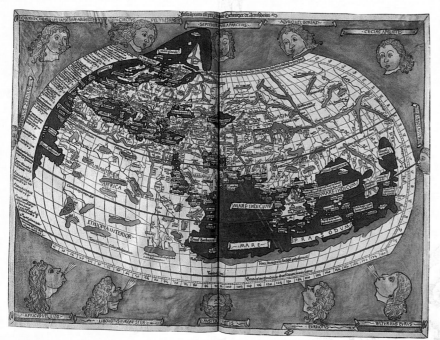

The background picture running across these pages is a map of the Netherlands drawn in 1658. Above, from the top, are a Babylonian clay tablet map dating from around 2500 B.C. and a medieval "T in O" map. The map on the left is a copy of Ptolemy's famous map of the world. The original was drawn in the second century A.D. This later copy was published in a German **atlas** in 1486.

Medieval Mapmakers

The mapmaking skills of the ancient Greeks didn't spread to the rest of Europe during the Middle Ages (A.D. 500 to A.D. 1500). World maps drawn in Europe at that time were very simple. Most of them are called "T in O" maps because of their shape. They show a T-shaped area of water separating the three continents of Europe, Africa, and Asia, all surrounded by a ring of ocean.

The great travelers and mapmakers of the Middle Ages were the Arabs and the Chinese. In the tenth century, the Arab explorer Al-Mas'udi of Baghdad produced a world map showing the Atlantic and Indian Oceans meeting south of Africa. This was a major development. Up to that time, most maps (including Ptolemy's) had shown the Indian Ocean completely surrounded by land.

In eastern Asia, Chinese cartographers were mapping their huge country and also their trade routes to India and the east coast of Africa. By 1155 they were producing printed maps–300 years before printed maps appeared in Europe.

The Scientific Age

In the late 1400s, the world entered the great age of exploration. In 1487 Bartolomeu Dias sailed around the tip of Africa. In 1492 Christopher Columbus landed in what would come to be called the Americas. In 1519 Ferdinand Magellan set out on his attempt to sail around the world. From the seventeenth century onward, methods of mapmaking and navigation improved rapidly. Accurate clocks and new instruments for star navigation enabled mapmakers to calculate latitude and longitude more precisely. While seafarers discovered new lands, overland expeditions mapped the interiors of North America, South America, Africa, and Australia, filling in our picture of the world.

Twentieth-century technology has provided mapmakers with many new tools. Laser and radar mapping instruments make quick work of measuring mountains. And photographs taken from satellites and aircraft allow even the most remote areas to be mapped in detail.

The picture below is a satellite view of part of Tennessee. Modern mapmakers use satellite photographs to make maps.

Peeling the Globe

Because the world is round, the only truly accurate map is a globe, which can show all the land and sea areas at the right size and shape and in their correct positions relative to one another. But as soon as we try to transfer the continents and oceans from the globe to a flat sheet of paper, we have a problem. The shapes, the sizes, or the positioning become distorted.

Mapmakers transfer the latitude and longitude grid from the globe to a flat sheet of paper using one of many map projections, each of which gives a different view of the world. Cartographers choose a map projection based on what that particular map is going to be used for.

There are two main families of map projections. The ones in the first group are based on the idea of "peeling" the globe in various ways. Peeling causes the grid to be broken–or interrupted–in places, and so these are called interrupted map projections. Uninterrupted map projections keep the grid unbroken but stretch it in various ways to fit the page. Uninterrupted projections are easier to look at, even though the shapes and sizes of the oceans and continents are distorted.

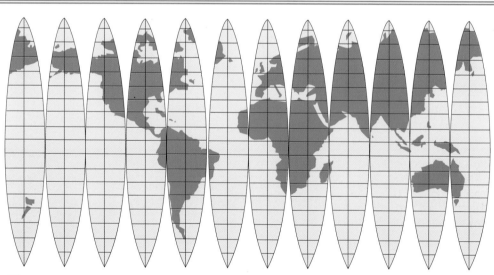

A Perfect Fit
A map of the world cut into 12 segments like this was first used nearly 500 years ago. It was not meant to be a flat map but rather was a covering for a wooden globe. This is a modern version, which you can use to make a pocket globe of your own.

Trace the map onto a sheet of paper and color in the land and sea areas. Then careful cut around the segments and glue the map onto a golf ball, taking care to smooth down each segment so that all the edges meet neatly. When the glue is dry, varnish the globe to protect the surface of the paper.

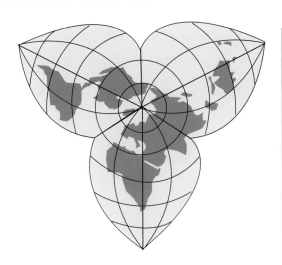

The tetrahedral projection looks down on the North Pole, with the earth's surface "peeled back" from the South Pole in three large sections. Shapes, sizes, and relative positions are all distorted.

Peel your own globe

Take a large orange and draw lines of latitude and longitude on it. Then roughly sketch in the continents. Take the peel off carefully, in one piece, and flatten it out. You will have to make a few extra small tears to get it to lie flat. Think about different ways of peeling the orange that might give a better result.

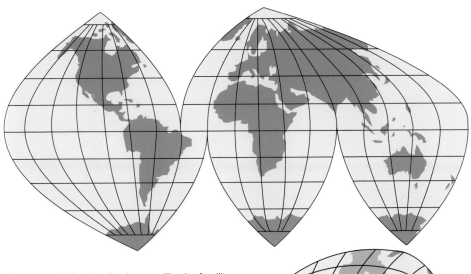

These examples show a wide variety of interrupted map projections. Compare them with the other family of maps on the next two pages.

The sinusoidal projection is more like the familiar maps in an atlas. The sizes of the land areas are accurate in relation to each other but the shapes get very distorted near the edges. Alaska, China, and Siberia are very squashed.

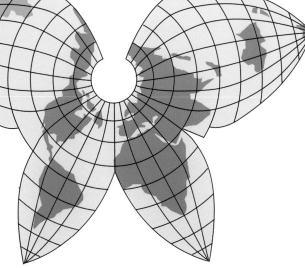

This more complicated four-leafed shape tries to balance reasonably accurate sizes and shapes with true angles and directions. The main areas are pretty good, but the Arctic is almost squeezed out, and the huge continent of Antarctica is just a few fragments at the "leaf" tips.

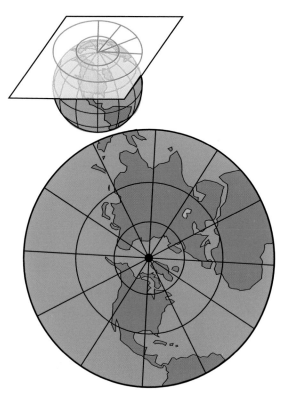

Flattening the Earth

The first map projections were made by shining a bright light through a glass globe marked with latitude and longitude lines. The light would cast, or project, the shadows of the lines onto a sheet of paper placed nearby, and the lines could then be traced with a pen to form a grid on the paper. (By the way, all the maps on this spread use uninterrupted projections.)

There are several hundred different map projections, but very few of them can be produced by the old-fashioned light method. Most of them are made with complicated mathematical formulas to work out exactly where each point on the globe should be placed on the map. Maps like these are usually drawn with the aid of computers.

Polar Azimuthal Projection
Azimuthal projections are made as if just one point on the paper is touching the globe. The point of contact, called the azimuth, is free of distortion. All directions and distances measured from the azimuth are accurate. Azimuthal projections are often used to map compact areas of the earth, such as the North Pole region (above left).

ACTIVITY

Project Your Own Grid

In this experiment, you can see how different azimuthal projections are made. Make half-globe "baskets" of latitude and longitude lines by shaping soft wire over a ball. Make one for a Northern or Southern Hemisphere, and another for an Eastern or Western Hemisphere.

Project the grid onto a sheet or a plain wall using a small, bright flashlight. If you place the flashlight bulb at the points shown here you will see how the grid changes. (In these drawings, part of a map has been added to show what it would look like in an atlas.)

A flashlight works well for the long-distance positions. A bulb on its own is best for the close-up projections.

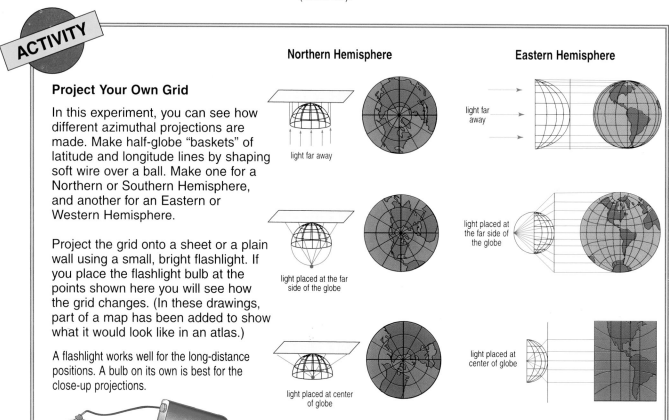

Northern Hemisphere   **Eastern Hemisphere**

light far away

light far away

light placed at the far side of the globe

light placed at the far side of the globe

light placed at center of globe

light placed at center of globe

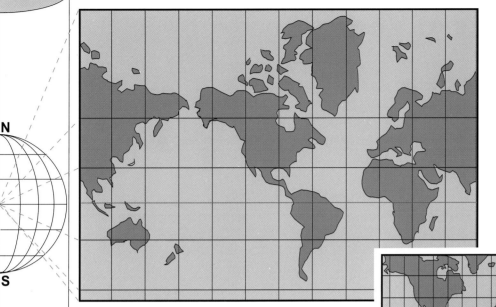

Mercator Projection
Mercator's is a cylindrical, conformal projection that has been modified to make it less distorted near the poles. Navigators use this projection because any route plotted as a straight line on the map can be followed from start to finish using the same compass direction.

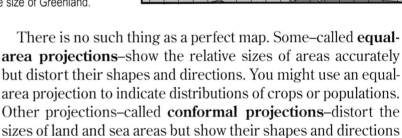

Cylindrical Projection
In this type, the light is at the center of the globe, and the grid is projected on to a sheet of paper wrapped around it to form a cylinder. There is no distortion at the equator, but the polar regions get very stretched. Cylindrical projections make Greenland look bigger than South America, when in fact South America is eight times the size of Greenland.

There is no such thing as a perfect map. Some–called **equal-area projections**–show the relative sizes of areas accurately but distort their shapes and directions. You might use an equal-area projection to indicate distributions of crops or populations. Other projections–called **conformal projections**–distort the sizes of land and sea areas but show their shapes and directions accurately. Navigators use conformal projection to plot courses.

The most common map projections are drawn as if a sheet of paper has been laid flat touching one point on the globe or has been wrapped around the globe to make a cone or a cylinder, which can then be unrolled and laid flat.

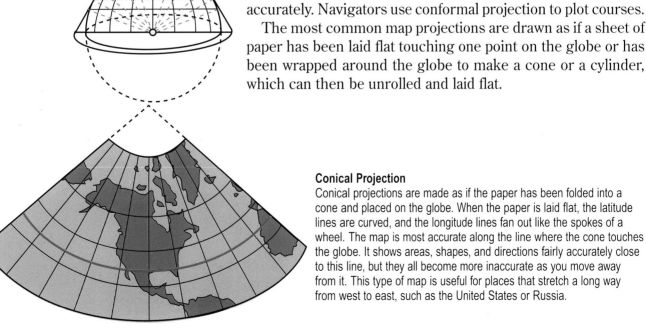

Conical Projection
Conical projections are made as if the paper has been folded into a cone and placed on the globe. When the paper is laid flat, the latitude lines are curved, and the longitude lines fan out like the spokes of a wheel. The map is most accurate along the line where the cone touches the globe. It shows areas, shapes, and directions fairly accurately close to this line, but they all become more inaccurate as you move away from it. This type of map is useful for places that stretch a long way from west to east, such as the United States or Russia.

Other Points of View

If you look at a plain ball, it has no top or bottom and no left or right side. The earth is slightly different because it is spinning around and around, and that movement gives it a top and bottom of sorts at the North and South Poles. But which is the top and which is the bottom? It is just a historical accident that we always put the North Pole at the top of globes and maps. The people who drew the first maps of the world lived in the northern half of the globe, so to them it seemed like north should face up. But to an astronomer far out in space, there would be no "right way up" for the earth.

Another historical accident explains why the lines of longitude are numbered from Greenwich, England. At the time the first world maps were drawn, English, Dutch, French, Spanish, and Portuguese seafarers were making their great voyages of exploration from western Europe, so a point in western Europe was chosen as the meridian. If the history of the world had been different, the prime meridian might have been drawn through New York, New York; Bombay, India; Cape Town, South Africa; or Sydney, Australia.

As the maps on these pages show, the way you see the world depends on who you are, and where you live. The maps might look strange, but they are not "wrong."

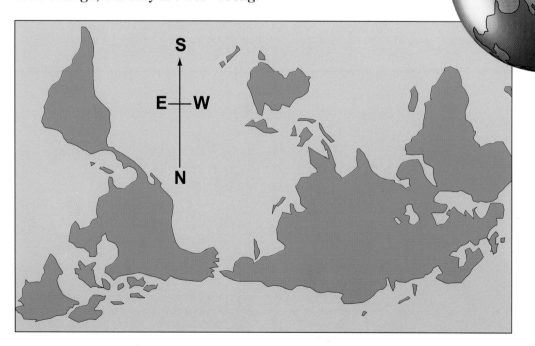

This unusual view of the world was produced in 1979 by an Australian named Stuart McArthur. Tired of jokes about Australia being "down under," he felt that the Northern Hemisphere countries had been "on top" for far too long. He may have just been making a point, but geographically his "south upward" map is just as correct as one with north at the top. We're just not used to it.

In the United States and Europe, world maps are usually drawn with the Greenwich meridian roughly in the middle. The Americas lie to the west, Europe and Africa are in the center, and Asia lies to the east. Mapmakers in some East Asian countries take a different view. They place the western Pacific Ocean in the center of their maps so their own countries are near the middle of the map. Europe and Africa lie to the west, and the Americas are to the east.

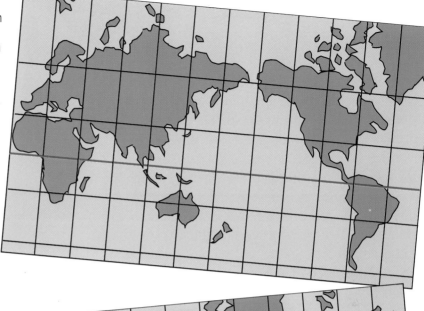

The world could be shown with the Americas in the middle, but the map is not very useful. Too much of it is taken up by ocean, and the vast land area of Asia is chopped in two and pushed out to the edges.

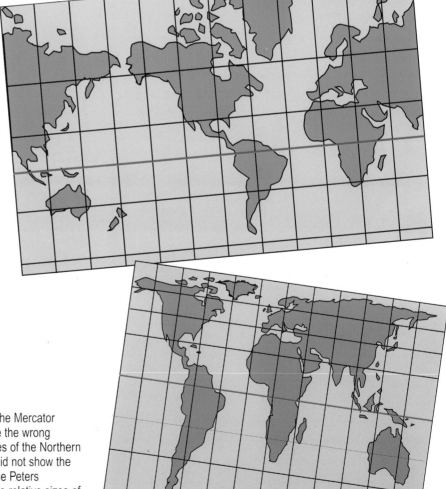

German mapmaker Arno Peters felt that the Mercator projection used for most world maps gave the wrong impression. It made the wealthier countries of the Northern Hemisphere look big and important and did not show the true size of the world's poorer regions. The Peters projection distorts shapes, but it shows the relative sizes of the countries accurately because it is based on the land area they cover.

Size, Distance, and Scale

One of the most important features of a map is its scale, which is a measure of how much of the real world is shown on the map. The scale tells you how many feet or miles of the earth's surface are represented by each inch on the map. (In countries that use the metric system, the scale indicates how many meters or kilometers are represented by each centimeter on the map.) Generally printed on the bottom of the map, the scale may be written out in words, such as "one inch equals one mile," or as a fraction 1/63,360 or a ratio 1:63,360. (Both mean 1 inch to 63,360 inches, which is one mile.) There is usually also a scale bar, which also helps measure distances on the map.

Small-scale maps show large areas of the earth's surface, such as states, countries, or even the whole world. They are called "small-scale" because their scale fraction—one divided by the scale number—is small. The bigger the scale number gets, the smaller the fraction becomes. Because small-scale maps depict large areas, they cannot give very much detail. But showing detail is not their job. Small-scale maps reveal the big picture. A world map with a scale of 1:80,000,000 could indicate soil types or rainfall or all the countries of the world. A scale of 1:4,000,000 would be more suitable for a map that presents the main cities, rivers, highways, and railroads of the United States.

For a tour of New England or some other U.S. region, you would want a large-scale map, such as a one-inch-to-a-mile map (1:63,360). This size would include small towns, minor roads, and local places of interest, as well as much more detail of the landscape.

Very large scales are used for town maps. At a scale of 1:20,000 (more than three inches of map for each mile), every street can be identified. At 1:10,000, every house can be shown.

How Far Is It?

To find the shortest distance between two towns, lay a strip of paper on the map with its edge touching the two towns. Make a mark on the paper against each town. Then place the paper strip against the scale bar, with the first mark next to the zero. Read the distance to the second mark off the scale bar.

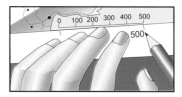

If your tick marks are too far apart for the scale bar, mark the end of the bar on the paper, noting how many miles it represents, then slide this mark back to the zero and measure off the remaining distance. Add together the two distances.

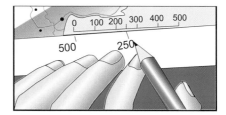

In this example, the distance from A to B is 500 miles plus 250 miles–that is, 750 miles.

It is often more useful to know the approximate distance by road. You can find that by laying a piece of string along the route and then measuring the string (pulled out straight) against the scale bar.

The easiest way of all is to use a route measurer. This neat little device has a small wheel that you roll along the route. The distance traveled can be read off the dial.

On most maps, the scale bar is marked off in both miles and kilometers. The first few main divisions are usually divided into smaller units to help you estimate distances more accurately.

The Mapmaker's Zoom Lens

Changing from a small-scale map to a large-scale map in stages is like being in a spacecraft and looking down at the earth through a powerful zoom lens. As you zoom in, the size of the area you can see gets smaller and smaller, but with every step you can see more and more detail.

Each of these maps has a scale roughly 10 times bigger than the one before it. If the series went on long enough, you could have a plan of Chicago's Soldier Field, home of the Chicago Bears football team, and even end up with a plan of the team's locker room.

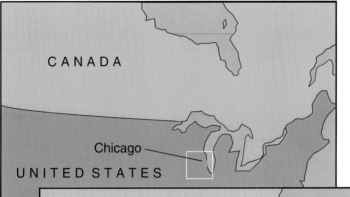

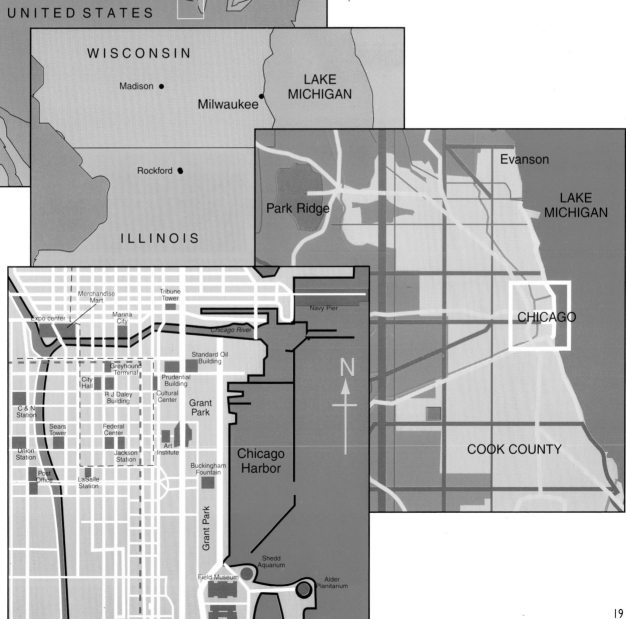

Where Are We?

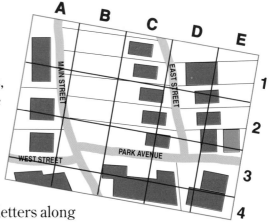

A good map can tell us a great deal about the roads, railroads, towns, and landscape of an area. But if the map is going to be really useful, we also need a way of giving exact positions so that we can tell someone precisely where we are.

The easiest way of fixing positions is by dividing the map into squares. On a map of a small area, like a shopping center, the squares are often identified by letters along the top of the map and numbers down the side. A key printed at the side of the map might then tell you that the information center is in square B4, the bus stops are in A2 and D5, and the snack bar is in F2. The sides of the square usually represent an easy walking distance, such as 100 yards.

On maps showing large areas of countryside, a similar but more accurate grid system works best. On these maps, lines–not squares–are numbered, and letters aren't used at all. Both sets of

Invitation

Come to a party on Friday night at John's house, E2 on the map.

Look at the top and right margins of this map of Boston, Massachusetts, and you will find three grid numbering systems! The figures in the corner show that the corner of the map is at longitude 71° 00' North and latitude 42° 22' 30" West. The numbers in feet relate to the Massachusetts state grid. And the combined small and large numbers (for example, ^{46}90) refer to the main USGS grid lines printed on the map.

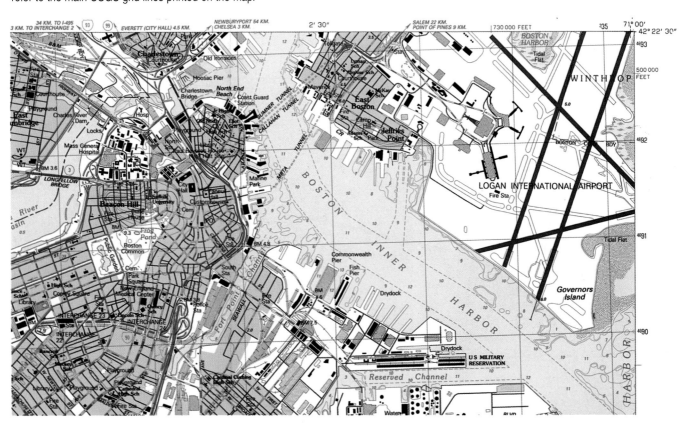

lines are given two-figure numbers. The numbers of the vertical lines increase as you move eastward (left to right) across the map, so these lines are called "eastings." The horizontal line numbers increase as you go northward (bottom to top), so these lines are called "northings." A square can be identified by the numbers of the lines that cross at the bottom left-hand (southwestern) corner. The first two numbers are the eastings, the second two are the northings, and together they are called the coordinates of the corner. For even greater accuracy, the square can be divided each way into tenths, making a very precise map reference.

☆☆☆☆☆☆☆☆☆☆☆☆☆

Here's a simple way of remembering how to use map coordinates. To find the place you are looking for, go "along the passage and up the stairs." That is read to the right first, then upward.

☆☆☆☆☆☆☆☆☆☆☆☆☆

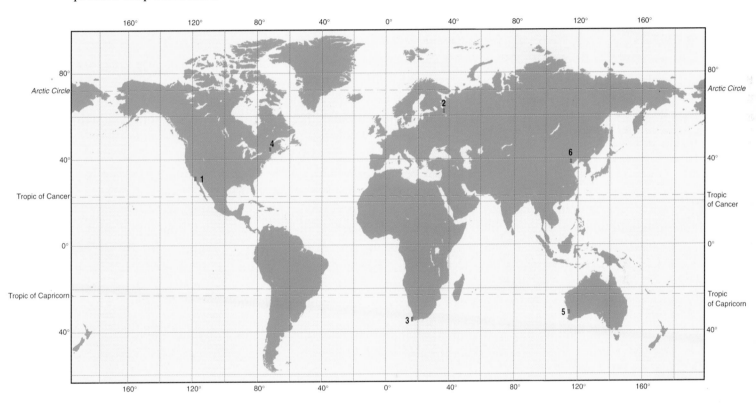

Using an Atlas

If you want to find a town, a river, or a mountain in an atlas, the quickest way is to go straight to the index. There you will find all the towns and named physical features listed alphabetically, along with where to find them. But you will also find that the positions are given in a slightly different way. Instead of giving eastings and northings, atlases give the latitude and longitude of each place, latitude first. Washington D.C., for example, lies 39 degrees north of the equator (39° N) and 77 degrees west of the Greenwich meridian (77° W). In most atlases, positions are given in degrees and minutes (sixtieths of a degree) for greater accuracy. Washington D.C. is at 38° 55'N, 77° 01'W.

Which cities are found at:
1. 34° N 118° W
2. 56° N 37° E
3. 34° S 18° E

What is the latitude and longitude of:
4. Ottawa, Canada
5. Perth, Australia
6. Beijing, China

You will find the answers on page 47.

The First Navigators
Chinese navigators used magnetic compasses more than 1,000 years ago. The devices were so reliable that Chinese traders were able to visit East Africa, which lay thousands of miles away.

Which Way Do I Go?

The most important aid to a traveler is a **compass**, because no matter where you are on the face of the globe, the compass will always point north. And as long as you know one direction accurately, you can figure out any other direction you need. In other words, you can navigate.

A magnetic compass consists of a pointer made of magnetized iron that is perched on top of a needle so that it can turn freely. The compass always points north because the earth behaves like a huge magnet, and the pointer automatically lines up with the earth's magnetic field. But we have to be careful with terms like north, because there is more than one north. The geographic North Pole is the northern end of the earth's axis–the imaginary line around which the earth turns. The geographic North Pole is also the point at which all the longitude lines meet. The North Magnetic Pole is about 870 miles away, because the earth's magnetic field is at a slight angle to the earth's axis. It is the North Magnetic Pole that the compass points to. In the Southern Hemisphere, the South Magnetic Pole is located 870 miles from the geographic South Pole in Antarctica. For most journeys, the difference between true north and magnetic north is not very important, but travelers in the Arctic and the Antarctic have to allow for it or they would soon find themselves way off course.

Overland travelers navigate using a combination of map coordinates, compass directions, and landmarks such as towns, hills, and rivers. Pilots flying above the clouds and sailors far out at sea have no landmarks to help them, and so they have a different system of coordinates. Instead of grid squares, they look at compass directions (**bearings**) and distances to plot their courses.

Magnetic Attraction
Invisible lines of magnetic force surround the earth. The compass needle is also a magnet, with its own south pole at one end and its north pole at the other. Two north magnetic poles will push one another away, but a south and a north attract one another. The south pole end of the needle is pulled toward the earth's North Magnetic Pole—and there it stays, in line with the force field.

You can make your own compass. First stroke a large sewing needle about 50 times with a magnet. (Always stroke in the same direction.) Then lay the needle on a flat piece of cork that is floating in a dish of water. The needle will swing around to north and will return there even if you turn the dish.

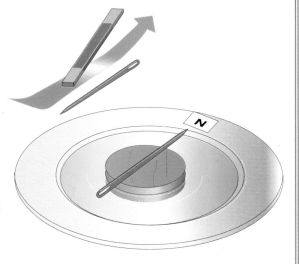

Lining Up North

Good maps usually have three north arrows printed on them. One shows true north (geographical north), one shows magnetic north, and the third shows grid north (the direction of the grid lines on the map). These hikers line up the magnetic north arrow on their map with the needle on their compass. This will line up their map with the landscape around them.

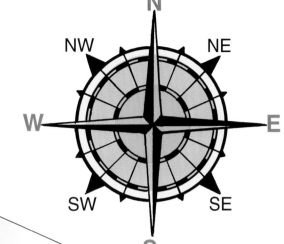

The points of the Compass

Compass directions can be given in words–north (N), southwest (SW), north-northeast (NNE), and so on. Compass directions can also be given as bearings, in numbers of degrees measured clockwise from the north line.

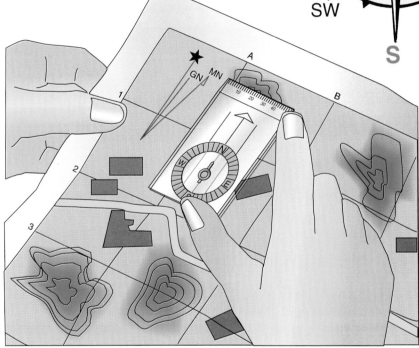

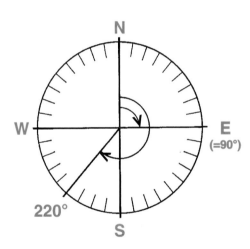

Heading for Nassau

On a direct line between Miami, Florida, and Nassau, the Bahamas, no land breaks the path. But the waters covering the reefs of the Great Bahama Bank along this path are only a few feet deep in places.

To be sure of a safe journey, the sailor plots a three-legged course through deeper waters between the reefs. The sailor must change the bearing (or heading) at least twice before reaching Nassau.

First Leg: 84 miles on a bearing of 65 degrees
Second Leg: 105 miles on a bearing of 110 degrees
Final Leg: About 45 miles on a bearing of 173 degrees

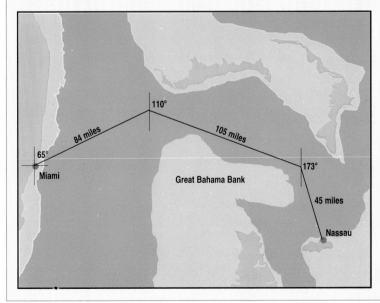

The Shape of the Land

When you look at a small-scale landscape map, the image resembles a three-dimensional (3-D) model that reveals mountains, river valleys, lowland plains, headlands, and bays. Geographers call this physical landscape **topography**, or relief.

Most small-scale maps use a relief map as a starting point, or base map. Other information such as towns, roads, national parks, and historic places can then be added on top. Large-scale maps such as town plans often ignore the relief and just show the streets and buildings laid out as if the land were flat.

Showing relief well is one of the most skillful parts of making a map. The height of a place, called its altitude or **elevation**, is its distance in feet above sea level (the average level of the water in the oceans, after accounting for the rise and fall of the tides). Special elevation points–for example, mountains, passes, and surveyors' reference points called spot heights–may have their actual heights marked on the map in numbers.

Colors or contour lines, which join places that are the same height above sea level, indicate other elevations. The best relief maps use a combination of methods, usually contour lines with color and shading on one side of the hills. The shading makes it appear as if the hills are lit by the sun, giving them a 3-D appearance.

Above: On very old maps, little pictures often identify hills and mountains. The pictures simply show that a line of hills exists at that place. They don't show the exact location, shape, or elevation.

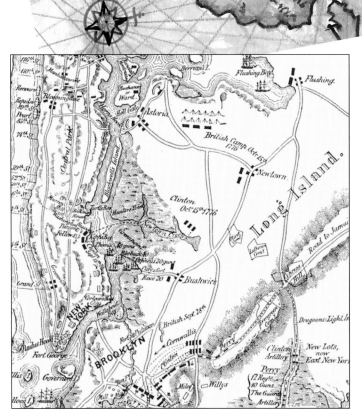

Left: Another method used on old maps is called hachuring. Straight lines fanning outward mark hills. To show steep slopes, the mapmaker draws the lines close together or makes them thick. The result is that steep slopes appear darker than gentle ones.

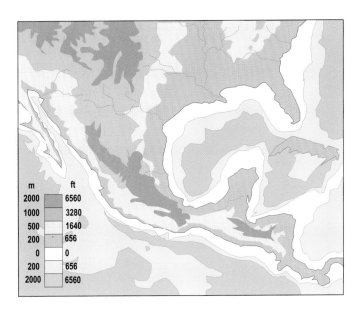

Small-scale maps usually show relief by color. Land between sea level and 500 feet might be pale green. Land between 500 and 1,500 feet may be yellow. Land between 1,500 and 3,000 feet may be light brown and so on. Mapmakers usually reserve gray and purple for the highest regions of mountain ranges. The depth of the sea can be shown in the same way. Shallow water is colored very pale blue, and the blue gets deeper as the water gets deeper. Maps of water depth are called bathymetric charts.

Contour lines give a very good picture of the shape of the land. All the points on a contour line are at the same height, so a small round hill will have circular lines running around it. The number of feet of altitude shown by each contour line will vary with the scale of the map. But the patterns they make will always be the same. Contours packed close together show steep hills. Wide-spaced contours show gently sloping land.

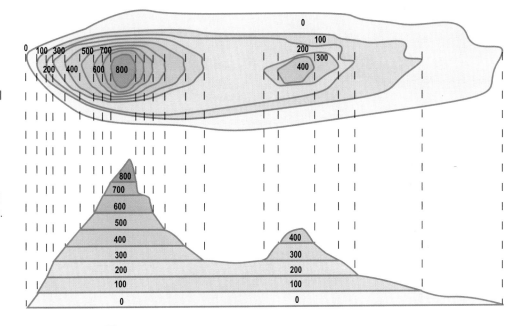

Look for V-shapes in the contours. The lines are numbered to show their heights. If the biggest numbers are on the outside of the V, the shape is a valley. If the biggest numbers are on the inside, the shape is a long narrow hill or spur. What do you think the contour lines of Crater Lake, Oregon, would look like?

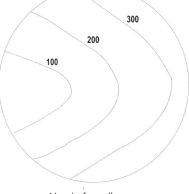

Head of a valley

Spur or ridge

Symbols and Keys

Map designers have to fit a lot of information into a very small space. To do this, they use colors and symbols to represent natural and artificial features. The colors and symbols are explained in the key. On U.S. Geological Survey maps, black is used for artificial objects such as tunnels, bridges, and buildings and also for most place names. Blue identifies rivers, lakes, and marshes. Brown is for contour lines, green is for vegetation, and red is for cities and some types of road.

Different types of maps require different symbols, but they must always be clear and easy to understand, even when they are printed very small. A dot or square with a cross on top usually symbolizes a church. A telephone receiver indicates a public telephone. A tent stands for a campsite, and small aircraft typically show the location of airports.

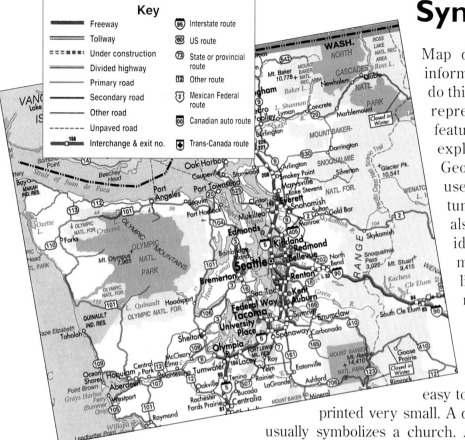

This professionally made map has a very detailed key that indicates how all the different types of roads are shown on the map.

Maps for younger readers have simple keys, but they can still provide a lot of information. This map tells us that North America has snow-covered mountains in the north and west and lower rounded ranges in the south. It also shows the band of coniferous forest in the north, the deciduous woodlands of the eastern states, the desert areas of the southwest, and the tropical vegetation of Central America.

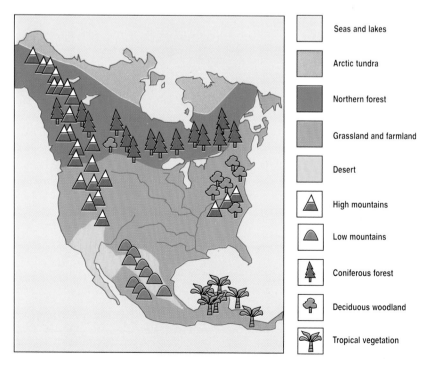

Seas and lakes

Arctic tundra

Northern forest

Grassland and farmland

Desert

High mountains

Low mountains

Coniferous forest

Deciduous woodland

Tropical vegetation

Map symbols also vary from country to country, but their meaning is usually clear because mapmakers worldwide follow the same basic rules. The thickest lines represent the most important roads, with their route numbers shown at regular intervals. Other symbols indicate whether a road is a tollway or a freeway.

The weather charts that meteorologists use are very different from the simplified maps we see in a TV weather forecast. Weather charts are covered with clusters of tiny symbols that summarize the weather at the reporting stations. Each cluster can show 20 or more pieces of information.

As well as showing where things are, map symbols can also answer questions like "How much?" and "What share?" Dot maps use a single dot to represent a quantity such as 1,000 people or 10,000 tons of potatoes. The more dots, the more people or potatoes there are. On other maps, the size or the color of the symbol provides information about quantity. And if the mapmaker wants to show the total size of a quantity and also how it is split up into different categories (such as the total amount of farmland and what it is used for), then pie charts and other graphics can be used.

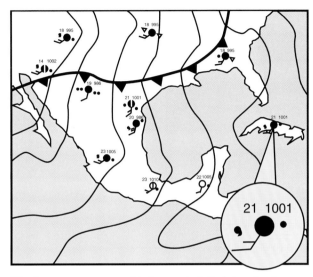

Weather maps are covered in tiny symbols that describe the cloud cover, wind speed and direction, air pressure, temperature, and current weather at each reporting station.

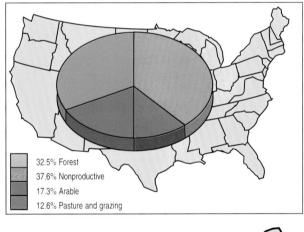

32.5% Forest
37.6% Nonproductive
17.3% Arable
12.6% Pasture and grazing

On the map to the right, the green dots provide two kinds of information about the production of industrial chemicals. The dots tell us where the chemicals are made, and the size of the dots shows the relative importance of the manufacturing centers. The pie chart above right indicates how much U.S. land is used for raising animals (pasture and grazing) and for growing crops (arable).

Major producer
Large producer
Medium producer
Small producer

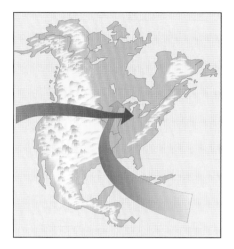

A weather forecaster might use a picture map to explain quickly and simply how tornadoes form.

Below: Shape distortion produces some very eye-catching maps. The world looks very different when mapmakers draw the land areas in proportion to the number of people who live there or in proportion to the quantity of goods they produce or buy. On this map of world oil production, you can see at a glance that most of Africa's oil comes from just two countries–Libya and Nigeria.

Information at a Glance

Some maps contain an enormous amount of information. Understanding them requires time and a close study of the keys and scales. The design of other maps provides a much smaller amount of information but quickly. You may only have to glance at the map for a second or two to learn what you need.

At-a-glance maps are a great help when time is short. For example, TV weather forecasters have only a few minutes to explain what the pressure and wind systems are doing and to tell us what tomorrow's weather is going to be like. Their maps are deliberately simple, with strong colors and big, bold symbols. News reports often have to cover stories about faraway places, and we need a quick reminder of where those places are. If the producer puts a simple location map on the screen for a moment, we know where we are and can concentrate on what the reporter is saying.

Drivers' strip maps show just the main highway, with all the entrances and exits marked, along with their route numbers, names of the nearest towns, details of reststops, and so on. The driver can see all the important information at a glance, quickly and safely, without having to stop and study a road atlas. Similar kinds of maps appear at bus and railroad stations to identify the different routes and services.

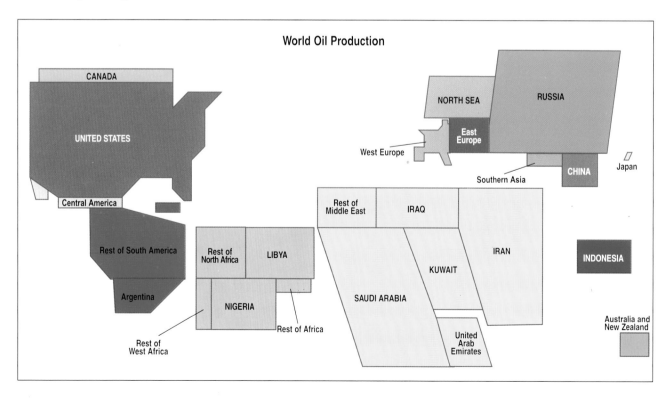

Patterns are often much easier to remember than lists of facts, so if a teacher is explaining where corn is grown in the United States, a dot distribution map can be a great help. Even without knowing exactly what each dot stands for, this kind of map instantly tells a story. Patterns of color are often used for climate information such as the amount of rain that falls each year. The strength of color indicates where most of the rain falls, and the key can tell you the exact amount.

Even the shapes of countries or continents can be distorted as a way of giving information. This type of map is most appropriate for making contrasts, between rich and poor countries, for example, or those that use most of the world's resources.

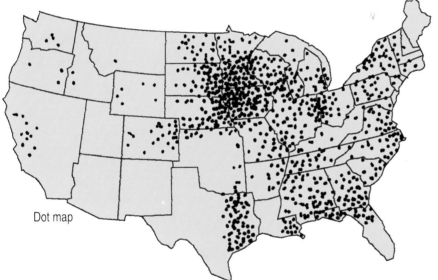

Dot map

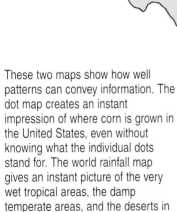

Many drivers' associations around the world publish strip maps of their countries' highways. The maps are useful on long trips because they highlight only the information needed for that particular journey. Some drivers make their own simple strip maps like the one above before setting out on a long trip.

These two maps show how well patterns can convey information. The dot map creates an instant impression of where corn is grown in the United States, even without knowing what the individual dots stand for. The world rainfall map gives an instant picture of the very wet tropical areas, the damp temperate areas, and the deserts in between.

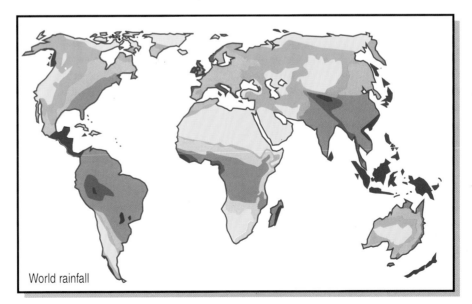

World rainfall

A Bird's-eye View

Imagine how the world looks to a mouse in your backyard. The mouse can't see very far because too many things block its view. Flowerbeds tower like forests, and a watering can is like a tall building. To a human, the view is very different. You can see over all these things, but a fence or a building will still block your view. You can see much more from an upstairs window and even more from a high-rise apartment. Imagine what the neighborhood looks like to a hawk hovering 200 feet in the air. The buildings and gardens are just flat squares and rectangles. The bird's-eye view is like a map.

Flying over the city in a helicopter enables police to look for traffic jams and to direct patrol cars to the scene of an accident quickly. A view from the air is also useful for following a criminal in a getaway car or on foot.

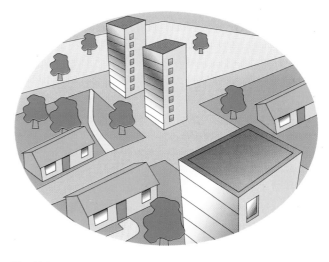

The higher you go, the more like a map your view becomes. A bird's-eye view is like looking at a map with a scale of 1:1.

ACTIVITY

A detailed map of a small area, such as a building or a single room, is called a plan. By drawing a scale plan–for example of your bedroom–you can experiment with different furniture arrangements without having to move anything around.

The first step is to choose a scale that enables you to fit the plan of your room on a sheet of paper. Measure the length and width of the room. If it's 10 feet long and 8 feet wide, a scale of 1 inch to 1 foot would be ideal, because the room plan would measure 10 inches by 8 inches. Take a sheet of paper and divide it into one-inch squares with fine pencil lines. This provides a grid for your plan. Draw in the outline of the room, to scale, and then measure and mark in the positions of the windows and also any pieces of furniture that can't be moved (such as a desk that is attached to the wall). Don't forget to mark the position of the door and the area that must be left clear so that the door can swing open.

Measure the length and width of each piece of furniture and add these to the plan in their current positions. If you want to rearrange the room, draw the pieces of furniture to scale on a separate sheet of paper and cut them out. You can then lay them on the plan and move them around to see what other arrangements might fit.

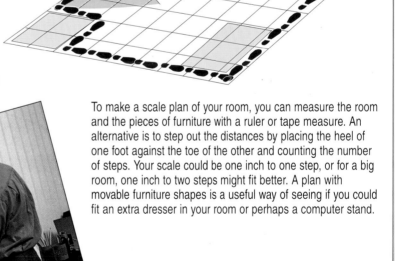

To make a scale plan of your room, you can measure the room and the pieces of furniture with a ruler or tape measure. An alternative is to step out the distances by placing the heel of one foot against the toe of the other and counting the number of steps. Your scale could be one inch to one step, or for a big room, one inch to two steps might fit better. A plan with movable furniture shapes is a useful way of seeing if you could fit an extra dresser in your room or perhaps a computer stand.

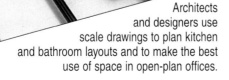

Architects and designers use scale drawings to plan kitchen and bathroom layouts and to make the best use of space in open-plan offices.

Making Your Own Map

To make a map of the neighborhood you live in, you will need a large sheet of paper, a ruler, pencils, a notebook in which to write down the measurements, and a compass. You will also need some way of measuring long distances. You can do this either by pacing them out or by making a measuring line.

The first job is to decide on a convenient scale, so pace out the longest distance you will want to show on your map. It might be from one end of your street to the other end. Let's say the total length is 200 yards. If your paper is big enough, you could choose a scale of 1 inch to 10 yards, making your finished map measure 20 inches across. Divide your paper into one-inch squares, ready for plotting your map. Each square on the map will represent 10 yards west to east and 10 yards north to south.

Choose as a starting point a convenient place, such as an intersection, near the center of the area you've chosen to map. Mark this point with a cross at the junction of two of the lines on your map grid.

Starting at the intersection, walk along the street counting the paces. When you come to the next intersection, stop and write down how many steps you have taken. Use simple notes such as

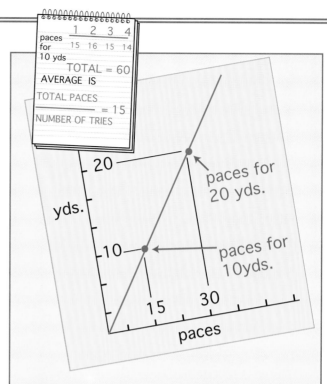

This chart shows you how to work out the average number of paces. Draw a line through the two points. Read off the yards value for any number of paces.

Pacing is quite accurate, and if you make a pacing graph you can convert paces to real measurements quickly and easily. Measure a distance of 10 yards, then pace it out several times using your normal walking pace. A simple calculation gives the average number of steps to cover 10 yards. Do the same for a measured 20 yards. Make a graph, using the test measurements to fix the position of the line.

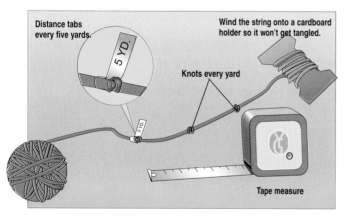

You can make a measuring line from string. Using a ruler or tape measure, put knots in the string one yard apart. Every five yards, make a tab from masking tape or adhesive labels. Write the distance on each tab to make counting easier. Starting with the highest mark, rewind the finished line onto a cardboard holder so the zero mark is at the free end.

"From start to corner of Main Street, 60 paces." Then continue, but don't forget to measure the width of the road you cross at the intersection. "Main Street, 20 paces wide." Then count the paces to the next intersection, and so on. When you reach the farthest point you want to map, go back home and draw in this first section of road on the grid. Then you can go back to your starting point and pace out the blocks going in each direction along Main Street. Take your time and build up the map one small section at a time.

If all the streets in your neighborhood are laid out at right angles to one another, mapping them will be easy. If some are at odd angles, you can still map them but you will need to use your compass and a **protractor** for drawing angles.

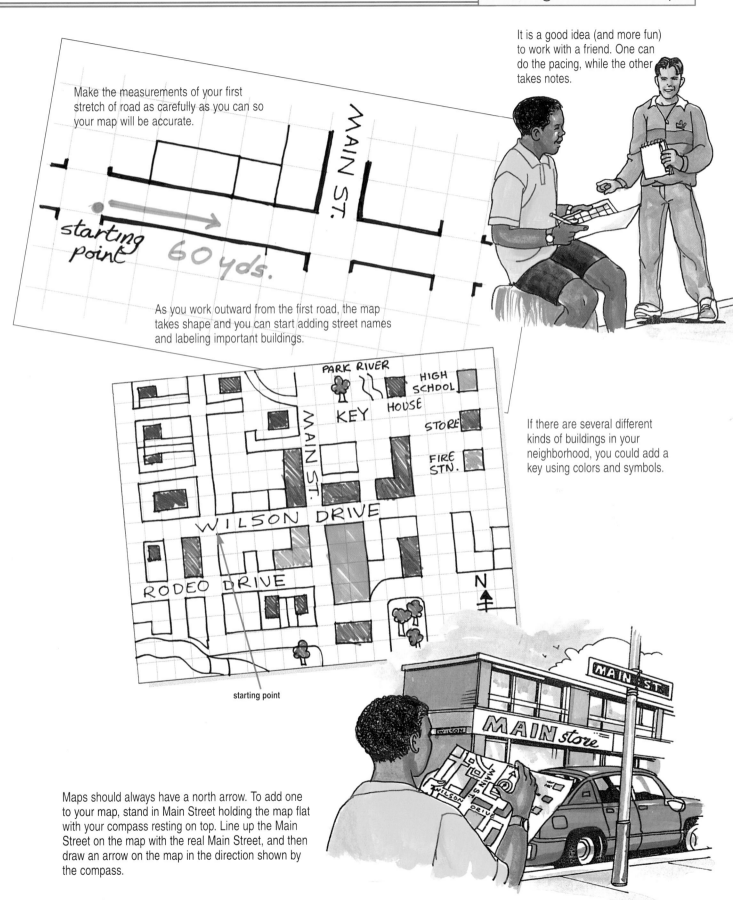

It is a good idea (and more fun) to work with a friend. One can do the pacing, while the other takes notes.

Make the measurements of your first stretch of road as carefully as you can so your map will be accurate.

MAIN ST.

starting point   60 yds.

As you work outward from the first road, the map takes shape and you can start adding street names and labeling important buildings.

PARK RIVER

KEY HOUSE

HIGH SCHOOL

STORE

FIRE STN.

MAIN ST.

WILSON DRIVE

RODEO DRIVE

N

starting point

If there are several different kinds of buildings in your neighborhood, you could add a key using colors and symbols.

MAIN store

Maps should always have a north arrow. To add one to your map, stand in Main Street holding the map flat with your compass resting on top. Line up the Main Street on the map with the real Main Street, and then draw an arrow on the map in the direction shown by the compass.

33

Surveying the Countryside

The previously described mapping method works well when all the roads are at right angles. But when some of the roads are not at right angles, you will need to measure their directions to plot them on your map. The simplest way is by making a **bearing board**. This simple device gives you a quick way of measuring the angle between two roads. You can then use a protractor to draw the road on your map at the correct angle.

Measuring angles is called making a plane table survey and is the main way of drawing maps in the countryside. You can try making one yourself. All you need is a drawing board, pencils, a bearing board, and a protractor. The map is drawn as you work, so you can check things as you go along. The first thing you need to do is set a baseline. This is an imaginary line between two places (base stations) that have good all-around views of the area you want to map. Hilltops, visitors' lookout points, church towers, and fire watchtowers are appropriate places to use. The base stations need to be a convenient distance apart–about a mile is good–and you need to know the distance accurately. You can get this information from a local map of the area. To make your own map, measure the angles to features in the landscape from several different points along the baseline. When these angles are plotted on the map they give the exact position of each feature you have surveyed.

Professional mapmakers use similar methods but with very high-tech instruments called theodolites. These are rather like a bearing board combined with a telescope that can be turned around to point in any direction. The telescope can also be tilted up and down so that it can measure vertical angles as well as horizontal ones. This allows the surveyor to measure the height of mountains and the depth of valleys. The most modern theodolites use a thin laser beam that can be bounced off a reflector several miles away. They are so accurate they can measure angles to one-six-hundredth of a degree.

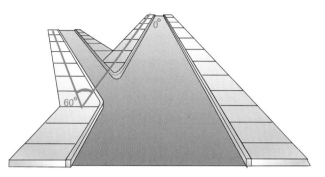

Imagine an angled side road off Main Street on the map on page 33. This is how you would survey it: Go to the site where the angled road intersects Main Street. Set the bearing board with the zero line pointing along Main Street. Then swing the bar around and sight it along the side road. Read off the angle shown by the pointer (60 degrees).

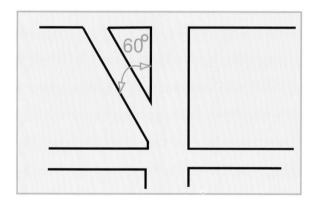

Use a protractor to measure the same angle off of Main Street on your map and draw in the side road.

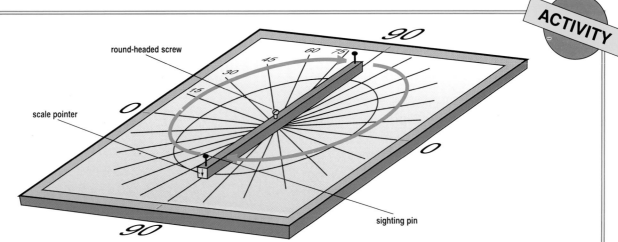

round-headed screw

scale pointer

90

60 75

45

30

15

0

0

90

sighting pin

Making a Bearing Board

To make a map, you often need to measure the angles between roads that don't cross at 90 degrees or between a baseline and a distant object like a mountain or a church steeple. The simplest way is to make bearing board.

Cover a one-foot-square wooden board with drawing paper. Use a ruler to mark the halfway points of the sides, then draw lines between them to form a cross. This gives you the center. With compasses, draw a large circle, then use a protractor to divide the circle into 15-degree segments. Put small tick marks on the circle at 1-degree intervals between the segment lines. Make a sighting bar from a piece of light wood (balsa is ideal). Fix it to the board with a nail or screw, just loose enough to swing around. Add sighting pins as shown in the drawing above.

To measure the angle between two roads, line up the zero line of the board with one road, then swing the sight bar around and aim it along the second road. Hold the bar so that it can't swing out of position, and read off the angle on the scale.

Right: Modern surveying instruments combine laser technology and computer technology. Instead of writing down all the readings, the surveyor lines up the theodolite and then simply presses a "Record" button. The angles are automatically stored in the instrument's own memory chip and can be downloaded straight into a computer back in the office.

Below: A mapping system called triangulation was invented in the sixteenth century. Like other forms of surveying it starts with a baseline but then builds up a series of triangles to fix positions of buildings and other features.

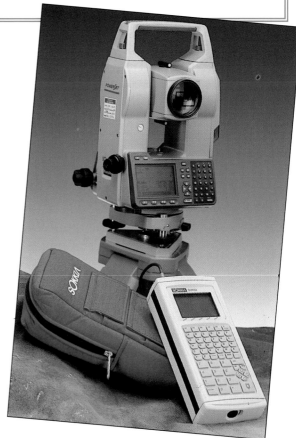

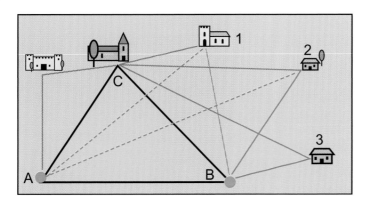

Making Maps by Hand

Although advanced technology is changing the way cartographers work, many maps are still produced by hand. But the first step in making any new map is to collect all the information (data) that will be shown. The type of information will depend on the kind of map the cartographer wants to create. Some of this information might come from other maps. Some might be from air or satellite photographs. Some might result from special surveys of the area, and some might come from government statistics.

When all the data has been gathered, the cartographer has to choose a suitable base map–the background map on which the other, more specialized information will be plotted. For vegetation maps, geology maps, and maps of river systems, the cartographer will usually want a contour base map that shows the shape of the ground. For maps indicating land use or industrial statistics, a base map that identifies major towns and state boundaries will help compare one area with another. The mapmaker creates the base map by placing a sheet of transparent material over a master map of the area and tracing only the needed features. If the new map is to be smaller than the master map, some of the detail may have to be simplified so that the new map is not too cluttered.

The cartographer plots by hand all the new information that is going to appear on the map on the base map and adds a new key and scale. A large camera then reduces the new map to its final size.

The map next goes through scribing, a tried-and-true process that produces the very sharp lines and symbols needed for high-quality printing. The map is laid on a light table and covered with a sheet of clear plastic with a colored coating. Using a fine cutting (scribing) tool, the cartographer removes the colored layer over the lines and symbols on the map, allowing the light to shine through. The plastic film then goes through a final photographic process to make the metal plates for the printing machines.

A cartographer uses a magnifier to check that all the lines on the coated plastic scribing sheet are clean and sharp. The smaller pictures, reading clockwise, show data being collected for a new map; a master film being checked; corrections being made to a film; and a light-sensitive printing plate being prepared in the darkroom.

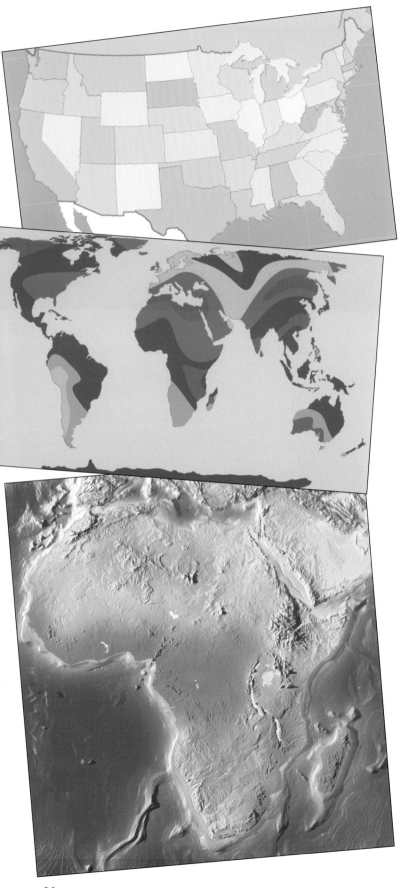

Mapmaking with Computers

Computers are great tools for mapmakers, because after all the basic information has been converted into a language the computer can understand, the computer can do almost anything with it. With the right cartographic software, the computer can draw a map showing just the roads or roads plus rivers and contour lines or even the size of last year's cotton crop. Better still the computer can do this with total accuracy and can enlarge or reduce sections of the map without spoiling the detail. To change the size of a hand-drawn map, the whole map has to be redrawn. The computer just needs new size instructions. It will then recalculate all the positions on the map, rescale everything, and even adjust the thickness of the lines to suit the new scale. Another huge advantage of using computers is that maps can be updated very quickly and easily. All you have to do is update the data files. The computer does the rest.

Before the computer can do anything, however, all the information has to be digitized–that is, converted into the binary code of zeros and ones that all computers use. Loading all the information into the computer is called data capture, and it can be done in two ways. The first is by using a digitizing table. The original map is laid out flat, and the operator follows each road and contour line in turn with a small device called a cursor, which is a lot like a computer mouse. Each time the button is clicked, the computer records the coordinates of the point on the map. The records for each road, river, contour line, and building are coded and filed separately. This method allows the computer to

separate them, if you want a map showing just the buildings and roads, or combine them, if you want to show the landscape features as well. The second data capture method requires no human work at all. The original map is fed through a machine called a scanner, which records the whole picture in digital form.

Pie charts and other graphics for showing statistical information are drawn using a separate graphics program. The computer operator can then display the map on a monitor and position the graphics using the main mapping program.

With enough computer memory to store the data and the right software to handle it, a cartographer can produce anything from a simple map of state boundaries to a relief map of the whole continent.

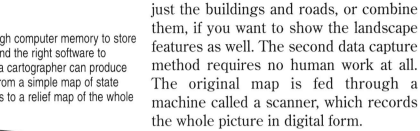

A great advantage of computer mapping is that after the database is complete, it is very easy to update whole maps or parts of them, and new maps can be produced at any size you want. Here a section of a road atlas is being checked and updated in preparation for printing a new edition.

Aerial Photography

Aerial surveying is one of the best methods of mapping very large areas, especially mountainous regions, deserts, or the Arctic wilderness, where it's difficult to get around on foot or with motor vehicles. A light aircraft equipped with special downward-pointing cameras flies back and forth along a series of parallel tracks, taking photographs continuously. The height of the aircraft and the frequency of the camera shots are adjusted so that the photographs overlap. This makes sure that each patch of ground appears on at least two photographs. Because the plane is moving, the two views will always be from slightly different angles.

When two of these photographs are placed side by side under a special stereo viewer, the ground appears in 3-D–just like looking down on a model of the earth's surface. The cartographer then uses a stereo plotter to record information from the photographs and store it in a computer. The plotter's cursor is a dot of light floating above the image of the ground, and the operator can move it in any direction. By keeping the dot of light in contact with the 3-D image of the ground, each cursor click records the height of that point as well as its position. When the whole photograph has been covered, the computer has a digital record of the hills and valleys stored in its memory, along with details of roads, rivers, and other features. The mapping software can then draw contour maps or even a panoramic view.

In addition to the digital data capture system, many stereo plotters also have a mechanical arm called a pantograph attached to the cursor. As the operator follows roads, rivers, and other features, the pen on the pantograph automatically draws the same shape on a drawing board next to the plotter.

The small picture below shows an air survey technician loading a film cassette into one of the specialized cameras on the plane. The large picture depicts an aerial view of the Thames River in London, England. The picture is made up of several overlapping photographs.

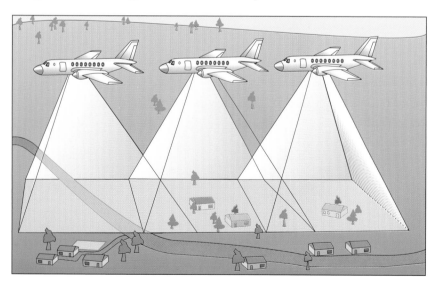

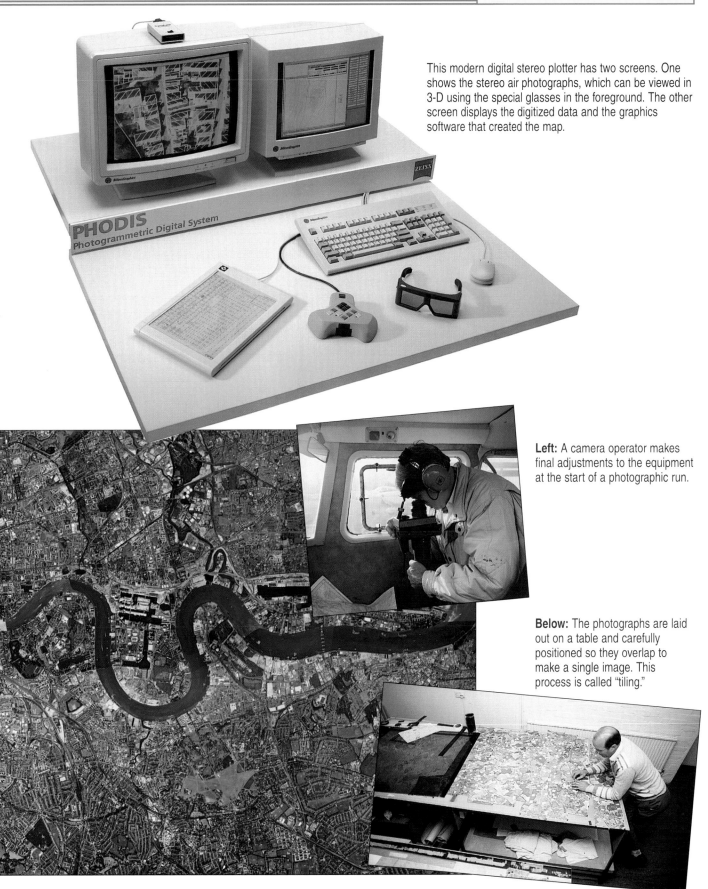

This modern digital stereo plotter has two screens. One shows the stereo air photographs, which can be viewed in 3-D using the special glasses in the foreground. The other screen displays the digitized data and the graphics software that created the map.

PHODIS
Photogrammetric Digital System

Left: A camera operator makes final adjustments to the equipment at the start of a photographic run.

Below: The photographs are laid out on a table and carefully positioned so they overlap to make a single image. This process is called "tiling."

Mapping by Satellite

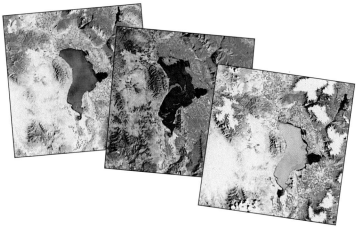

When a young Austrian named Philip Apian made a map of southern Germany in the sixteenth century it took him more than six years. These days a satellite can photograph the entire surface of the earth in just 18 days.

Modern satellites carry several different types of camera. Some work like ordinary cameras and take pictures using the light of the sun reflected off the earth's surface. Others bounce microwave radar beams off the surface and use the reflected beams to build up an image of the land. A third type

Above: Utah Lake, south of Salt Lake City, changes dramatically throughout the year. In autumn the lake is clear and dark. In summer it has red patches of algae on the surface. And in spring it is turned milky white by the fine rock dust washed down from the mountains by melting snow.

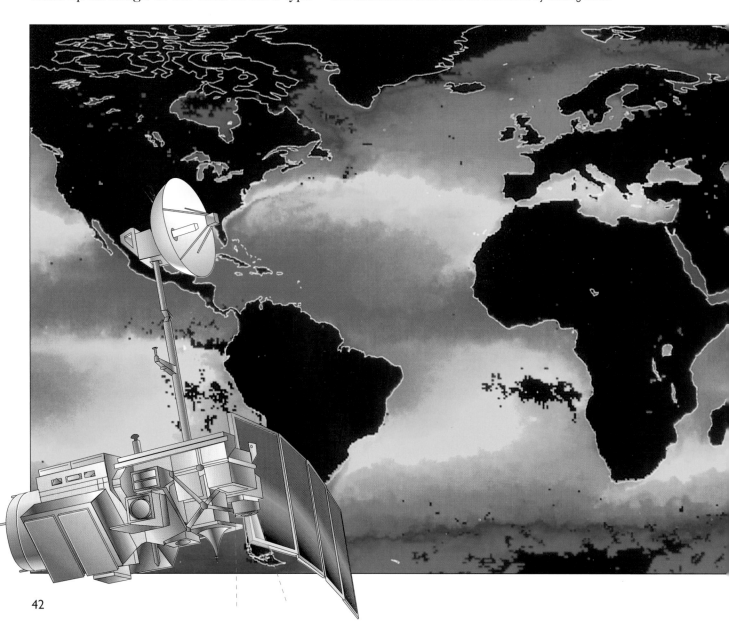

Above: This false-color photograph taken from the Earth Resources Technology Satellite (ERTS-1) shows the New York–New Jersey area. Red represents vegetation; built-up areas are pale blue; asphalt roads show as dark blue lines; and concrete roads and buildings appear white.

creates images of the earth by recording the different amounts of infrared radiation (heat) given off by water, rocks, and various kinds of vegetation.

Satellite photographs of cloud patterns are tools for weather forecasters and give early warning of hurricanes. Pictures of Antarctica have enabled scientists to chart the yearly freezing and melting of the Southern Ocean. Special sensors have made it possible to map the ozone hole in the atmosphere over Antarctica. And radar can "see" through cloud layers and map tropical areas, such as those in the Amazon Basin and parts of Southeast Asia.

Light is made up of many different colors. By analyzing how much of each color is being reflected, scientists can identify different types of vegetation. Using this method, maps can show areas of forest, grassland, and farmland. It is even possible to make maps indicating where forests have been burned or cut down or where crops are suffering from drought or diseases.

Heat-sensing instruments can map the warm and cold currents in the oceans and the spread of pollution from industrial areas. This kind of satellite mapping has revealed how much of South America's tropical rain forest has been destroyed by burning.

These different methods of gathering information–together known as remote sensing–have enabled cartographers to create maps of the earth that were impossible to produce in the 1960s.

Left: Satellites can even measure the temperature of the sea! This picture of the October pattern of sea surface temperatures was taken by the European Remote Sensing Satellite (ERS-1).

Making Maps and Globes

When you look at a map in an atlas, you see a whole range of colors. But it's all a trick of the printing process. If you look at a section of the map through a magnifying glass, all you'll see are dots of black, red, yellow, and blue ink–the four printing colors. The dots are so small that your eye doesn't pick them out at normal viewing distance. They merge together to give the appearance of different colors. There are no greens on the map, just mixtures of yellow and blue dots!

The dots are produced by processes called separation and screening, which are done after the new map has been created and checked. Scanners separate the picture of the map into four separate pictures–one in each of the four printing colors. The pictures are photographed through a fine mesh called a screen, which breaks up the image into dots. Each master film, with its pattern of dots, is then placed on a sheet of metal with a light-sensitive coating. Bright light is shone onto the metal, a process that hardens the coating on the areas that will print the map. These printing plates are then treated with other chemicals so that ink will stick to them only in the areas where ink is needed. The plates are then fixed to the big rollers of the printing press, and printing can begin.

The normal printing process uses just four ink colors–red, yellow, blue, and black. All the greens, browns, oranges, and purples you see on a map are created by tiny dots of these four colors mixed together in various proportions. On some high-quality maps and atlases extra colors give richer tones and special effects such as silver or gold.

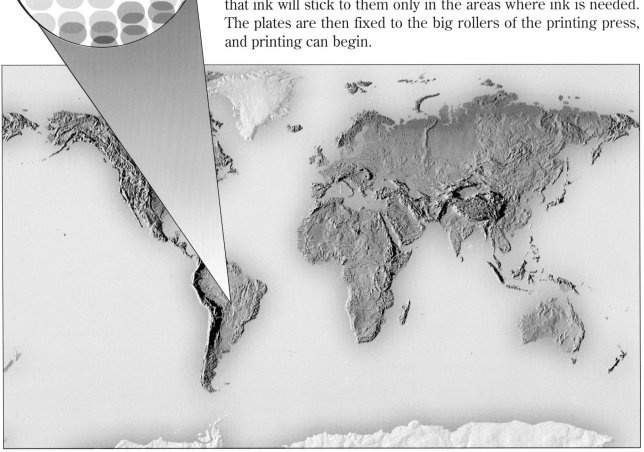

Right: In the assembly department, a technician checks that the thin printed plastic hemisphere is fitted snugly onto the hard plastic ball that gives the globe its strength. The next stages will be to match up the two halves of the globe, insert the axis rod, and mount the globe on its stand.

Above: Half-globes go down the production line from the molding section. Here a combination of heat and pressure has turned a strangely distorted map printed on a flat sheet of plastic into a true-to-life map of one of the earth's hemispheres.

Globes used to be made by first printing the map on paper as a strip of segments called gores that were then cut out and stuck onto a papier-mâché globe. It was very tricky work with so many edges to match up.

Modern globes are made by first printing the map on a flat sheet of flexible plastic. The map projection is a polar azimuthal version that is specially distorted so the plastic map can be heated and molded into a half-globe (hemisphere). When the half-globe cools, the plastic sets and is then fitted over a hard plastic ball for extra strength. Unlike the old-style globes with their many joined edges, the modern plastic globe has only a single seam, running around the equator.

Glossary

atlas: A book consisting mainly of maps.

azimuthal projection: A map projection in which the map is transferred to a sheet of paper that touches the globe at a single point.

bearing: The compass direction of one place from another.

bearing board: A simple device for measuring the angle between two features on the earth's surface.

cartographer: A person who makes maps.

compass: A device that indicates the direction of Magnetic North by means of a magnetized pointer.

conformal projection: A map projection in which the angles between places on the map are shown correctly.

elevation: The height of a place above mean sea level.

equal-area projection: A map projection that gives the land area on a map the same area as it has on a globe.

grid: A network of lines on a map, usually running north-south and east-west, used for giving positions.

key: A list of colors and symbols with a description of what each one stands for on the map.

latitude: The distance north or south of the equator, measured as an angle from the center of the earth. Lines of latitude encircle the earth parallel to the equator and are also called parallels.

longitude: The distance east or west of a line running through Greenwich, London. Lines of longitude encircle the earth from north to south, passing through the North and South Poles. The lines are also called meridians.

map projection: A way of representing the curved surface of the earth on a flat sheet of paper. There are many different map projections, but all distort the world in some way. The only perfect map is a globe.

protractor: A drawing instrument used for measuring angles.

scale: The relationship between distance on a map and the true distance on the earth's surface. In other words, how much of the earth's surface is represented by each inch of the map. A small-scale map shows a large area of the earth without giving much detail. A large-scale map shows a small area but in much more detail.

topography: The shape of the land surface. Also called relief.

Answers to Questions

Page 21

1. Los Angeles, California
2. Moscow, Russia
3. Cape Town, South Africa

4. 45° N 76° W
5. 32° S 116° E
6. 40° N 116° E